How Come No One Knew I Wanted to DIE!

DANITA BECKWORTH

Fulton Books
Meadville, PA

Published by Fulton Books 2024

ISBN 979-8-89427-219-1 (paperback)
ISBN 979-8-89427-220-7 (digital)

Printed in the United States of America

I was born on December 10, 1966. I grew up to trial and error. That is pretty much how I learned what to do and not what to do. My father was an alcoholic, and so was my mom. I lost my mom to alcohol when I was six years old, and I lost my dad when I was forty-five years old.

I was not taught how to love; I had to learn how to love. I was a very curious child. I remember my mom being abused by my dad. I remember her stabbing him because of the abuse, and he never hit her again.

I started trying things at age twelve, like putting grass out of the yard into some notebook paper and trying to smoke it. The grass was dried up and brown. It choked me so bad. That was the start of my addiction. By the time I was fifteen, I had started drinking what, at that time, was called malt liquor, and I was smoking marijuana. I continued doing that for years. My addiction got worse over time.

I started using powdered cocaine along with the beer and marijuana. I was always a curious person, so I tried what I would see other people do. I began to put the pow der and marijuana together, roll it up, and smoke it, not knowing how bad my addiction would keep growing. By this time, I had gotten pregnant at age seventeen with my first child. I dropped out of school to care for my child. Later on in life, in 1995, I got my high school diploma.

At age twenty-one, I had my second child. By this time, I had started using crack cocaine. I did not use it while being pregnant with my son, but I smoked crack cocaine while carrying my daughter. I thank God nothing happened to her.

After giving birth to my daughter, I started smoking crack cocaine almost every day, as long as I had the funds. I only got worse from there. I would have a lot of good days and a lot of bad days. On my good days, I would be that mom who taught my kids right from wrong. And then there would be days when I would go on a binge for days.

I would always manage to call my sister to get my kids. I had a lot of days when I would think about jumping off a bridge. But I never did. It would be so bad. I remember having bad, abusive relationships and staying in them because I did not know it was okay to leave. I didn't know what love was like. *It felt like love*, I thought.

Be talked to rough was what I heard from my daddy. He always said things like, "You stupid, ain't none of my children gonna be shit." I was used to hearing that. Yelling is all I remembered. I don't ever remember being told, "I love you."

I do remember my mom visiting me in the hospital when I was sick at four years old. I also remember her taking me to the bar with her. She would always tell me to stand outside the bar until she came out. That is pretty much all I remember until she died when I was six.

I remember pulling the gurney, not wanting them to take my mommy. I remember her funeral, but they would not let me go to the burial. That is my memory of my mommy. For years and years, I carried feelings with me of wanting to call someone Mom. Even wanting someone to act like a mom. All my life, I carried different feelings without even knowing how to talk about them.

I continued using drugs daily and doing whatever I had to do to get them. The only reason I did not stick a needle in my arm is because I am scared of needles to this day. My addiction was anything that got me high. If someone died, I would use it as a reason to get high. If a relationship did not work, I used it as an excuse to get high. It was a sick cycle. I wanted to quit, but I could not.

I remember praying in the crack house, asking God for help, and people would look at me as though I was crazy. I wanted to be a mother so bad, but being on crack cocaine won't let you do anything but stay high. I did a lot of things that I am not proud of. My kids needed me a lot, and I was absent; I was back and forth in their lives.

I remember being in an abusive relationship with this guy who destroyed everything in my apartment, even my kids' clothes and mine. I remember using that as an excuse to get high once again. I would call my sister to get my babies, and I would go on a binge. Me and my kids end up in the Hubbard House from the abuse. It only got worse from there.

We stayed there for days. Until one day, I left them in the Hubbard House by themselves, which is something I had never done. Before I got to this point, I had tried getting clean three times. Each time I tried, it was because my family wanted me to, or I was doing it because of my kids. I was not successful either time.

I have been in jail a couple of times and also in institutions three times. The time that I left my kids at the Hubbard House, I did not know it was the start of a better life for me. During that time, I was also in an abusive relationship. In the meantime, God was always there with me.

The lady at the Hubbard House said to me that my kids were so well groomed and well-mannered that she knew they did not belong in the system, so she did not call the police. She called my family. I did have to go see the judge, though. The judge asked me where I wanted my kids to go, and I said I wanted my son to be with my sister and my daughter with her grandmother.

I was Baker Acted by my sister. I was angry at first, but that is what saved my life. I was instructed by the judge to go to rehab as an inpatient for six months. I also had to take parenting classes while in treatment. I was serious about my recovery.

It turned out to be what I needed. They told me in a group session that usually only one or two people make it out and stay clean. I remember saying, "Well, that one person is going to be me."

After treatment, I got out and started doing what I was instructed to do by the judge. I was going to parenting classes and completing drug rehab while in rehab. I remember one time I had to take a urine test, and I knew I had been clean for a while. My test came back positive. There was a lady who used to work there whom I knew was jealous of me. I believe to this day that she put something in my urine. She was a worker who was also in recovery.

I survived treatment, and she did not. I have been clean for twenty-four years as of October 5, 2024. God never left me at that time. I did have support from a friend who was there during my jail time and treatment time and helped me with my kids. He was a man of his word. He was not abusive to me. He showed me what it was like to have a man who loved you. He passed away on August 18, 2018. He gave me the best life along with my kids. He always made sure we had a place to live and a car to drive.

Like I always said, he loved me and all my mess. In early recovery, I started doing research like family trees to try and find out where my addiction came from. It pointed out a lot of answers for me. I was also going to meetings for addicts and talking and listening to their stories, which gave me a lot of hope. They were just like me. I was always serious about my recovery once God gave it to me. There was still a lot of work in me that needed to be done.

After finally having a decent man in my life, I still did not have what it takes to not let a man mistreat me. I did not know I was still looking for love that I did not get from home. I met my new husband in December 2008. We got married in April 2009. He asked me to marry him thirteen days after we met.

I did get a sponsor while in one of the meetings. Her story was a lot like mine, and she did not use it as an excuse to get high, so I went up to her and asked, "Will you be my sponsor?" She said, "Yes, start doing recovery work."

We started with the first step shortly after I met her. By that time, I was so desperate to learn how to live life on life's terms. I was so open-minded in talking about all the bad things I had done 'til I asked her if it was a thing for being too open-minded. She said to me, "No, sweetie, it's a blessing to be that way."

By this time, I was open-minded, but I still had low self-esteem, no boundaries, and no love for myself. The year I married my husband was 2009. I met him in a club/restaurant in 2008. It was December, and he seemed to be a nice man that day. He asked me to be his wife thirteen days after we met. He would open the car door and close it for me when we would go on outings. I still had low self-esteem, no boundaries, and no love for myself. I spent years and years looking for happiness when I met my new husband.

I had a male friend staying at my house who used to be my lover and helped me raise my two kids. We did still have a real friendship. He was ill at the time. Our friendship was strong, but he never asked for my hand in marriage.

As time went on, I wanted to be a wife while I was still vibrant. I met my now-husband. Remember, I still had to learn who he was. I was this open-minded woman, thinking it was okay to take him by my house to prove to him that he meant a lot to me. And little did I know, it was the start of me seeing who he was at the time.

I did not want my friend, who was at the house. I wanted my now-husband. My friend, who was staying at the house, was just my friend. We had no love life, just friendship. He taught me the real meaning of friendship, and he was a confident man. He cared enough about me to school me about men, and he was one himself.

After trying to show my now-husband that all I wanted was him, he got violent with me for the first time. After growing up and knowing what my daddy used to do to my mother, I immediately stood up for myself.

All my life, I remember always meeting a violent man at some point. I'm still looking for love, though I don't know what to look for in a man or if I should be looking. My life was trial and error. I went through a lot in my marriage for about ten years. I have gone to jail, been on probation, and even got so depressed that I checked into a mental rehab.

I have left my husband a couple of times. The last time I left my husband, it was necessary. I started living on my own, like we were never going to get back together. I got my own place. Before I left my husband, we had gotten an eviction. Doing this time, he had a heart attack, and we were homeless to the point of staying in the hospital and staying at rehabs, which were our place of living because we had nowhere to go.

By this time, I had split from my husband and got my own place. What I learned in recovery was to vent on a daily basis and talk about what was inside my spirit. I got very good at that, and by this time, I am twenty-three years clean.

Being open-minded has become a part of my life. I had learned how to live life on life's terms without the use of drugs. After I left my husband, I had to stay with a good friend for about three months until my new apartment would be finished being built. I started going to church faithfully and learning my Bible. In doing that, God gave me self-esteem, boundaries, and love for myself.

I felt like God had given me what I was missing all the time. When I moved into my new apartment, I was happy. I did often miss my husband. I would see him ride through the parking lot to see if a car was in my parking spot (lol).

Until one day, he finally called and asked me if he could come over, and I said, "Yes, of course." By this time, I had started getting new furniture. He didn't seem too happy about it; we did end up arguing.

That day didn't go as planned. The next time he came over, he said to me, "I ain't leaving," and I said to him, "Well, you must be coming to do the right thing."

After the separation, I had self-esteem, love for myself, and boundaries. And I was ready to conquer anything. Me and my husband lived in that apartment for three years. My husband had let God do some work in him so he could be the man I married. God also did work in me. We both finally realized we wanted to be together forever. My husband applied for his disability, and he was 100 percent service-relaxed. We both applied for a new house and moved into our brand-new house in November 2023. We are at a point in our marriage where we allow each other to be who we are, and if there are necessary changes, we make them. We had also gotten better at communication.

Out of everything in this book, I have learned to be open-minded daily and vent when I need to, which is daily. Today, I pay attention to people, even if they say I have a headache, because there are so many suicides going on in this world. And people are saying they showed no signs; yes, they did. Pay attention. Stop being too busy because bills, etc., need to be paid. It is called life on life's terms. Get out of yourselves and go do better on purpose.

After being told that I was crazy and stupid, I have learned that those were just hurtful words and that I do not have to accept that kind of behavior from anyone. I have learned that abuse can come from anyone. I have learned that abuse can come spiritually, physically, and emotionally.

I do believe that everything I have experienced is for me to use it to help someone else who is going through it or may have already experienced it. I may already be walking in it now because I find myself talking to people about their trials and tribulations, trying to give them hope. I speak about what I have gone through to give them some hope. They look at me, and it seems to give them hope. I believe it helps to share my experiences, so they know they are not alone. Most of them, when I share, they believe I went through all I shared.

I have also learned how to live life on life's terms by not using an excuse to go get high off drugs anymore. If someone dies or things don't go like I think they should, I have learned that it will pass, and it is just a feeling. I have done the work through counseling to find my social happiness and my usefulness in life.

My life was trial and error, not just for me, but to use it to be a light to others. I am no longer a curious child; I am a smart woman now. I have accepted everything that I allowed to happen to me, and I have also forgiven a lot of wrong that was done to me in my life. Today I do realize that my dad and my mom both had issues that only God could fix and not me.

I now know how to love people, including myself and my children. It took some time for me to give in to my husband. I thank God I am finally happy in my marriage. I have also learned that I do not have to be talked to in any kind of way. I have also learned that I don't have to put up with mistreatment of any kind. Today, instead of drinking beer or alcohol, I drink apple cider or Welch's grape juice. I make sure I do not put anything in my body that is mood-altering or is addicting. I am very protective of my recovery.

I no longer try what I know is bad for me. I don't allow myself to be influenced. My kids have forgiven me for the past, and that means a lot to me. They often tell me how proud they are of me. I did get my real estate license and started doing real estate for seven years. I also completed cosmetology school. Those were a few goals I set once I got out of drug rehab.

Today, I look at life everyday as a good day compared to my past. It feels good to wake up every day not being high from drugs and being able to be a good mom and wife. I realize that today I teach my kids that mistakes happen in life, but they do not have to stay in them. They can make it regardless of what comes their way.

I used to talk my way up on the bridge almost every day, and I never made it there to jump off of it. Today, I drive across that same bridge and thank God every time that I am here to tell my story because God gave me self-esteem, boundaries, and love for myself. Those three things help me make it through life. I carry it with me every day.

Every day is a good day, is my cliche. Out of everything I have talked about in this book, I want people in the world to start paying attention to their loved ones, whether they are using drugs, depressed, or whatever the case may be. We can help save a person's life if we stop being so caught up in just our own lives.

There is someone who always needs us. Life is about paying bills and maintaining ourselves. *But* what about the people who are struggling day-to-day like I was? Many days in struggle, I wanted to die, and no one knew. That is the story that I hear a lot from people who are struggling. Please pay attention and love them until they can love themselves. Nobody came into this world in elementary school and said, "I want to be a drug addict; I want to struggle." Whatever the case is, please offer help.

It would make all the difference. If it weren't for people in my family helping me, I probably would not be here. They loved me until I could love myself. I have also learned that when a person knows better, they will do better.

I did get a chance to talk to my mom in counseling, in a circle, as though she was there. And it helped me to live better when Mother's Day came. I got a chance to ask things like why she left me and to tell her how much I missed her. That was a new beginning for me. I started living life and doing things on Mother's Day, like taking myself shopping and doing things she would be proud of. That is how I learned to stay connected and do what she would be proud of. With almost twenty-four years of being clean and free from drugs, life is great.

Life is great now. I wake up in the morning not feeling guilty from the night before. I thank God daily.

I am feeling like a proud mom today and a proud granny. I have six grandbabies. I love them so very much. It is like loving them and teaching them how not to go where I have been. I use all my wisdom and knowledge with my kids and grandkids. I no longer have to stay in the Hubbard House; I have my own house now. Life feels the way it should feel now that I am free of drugs and abuse. Today I tell myself that I am somebody, I am a queen, and I am worthy of doing anything. Today I am a present parent, grandmother, and wife. I show up today when I suppose to. I am responsible.

I often say to people and myself that I do believe my trials and tribulations were necessary in order for me to be molded into the woman that I am. I also have learned to pick my battles in my marriage and know when to walk away to calm down, so when we talk, there will be no yelling at one another.

As I look back at my past, I realize that God was always there with me. I would be the one to always leave, not God. Today, I gave God some time. I read scripture daily. It keeps me in a good mindset. I have so much today to be grateful and thankful for. I get excited when I have to tell my story to someone that I run across when I am out and about.

God is everything I need. With God's connection, there is nothing but happiness and accomplishment. Today I choose to take life one moment at a time and know when to give myself a break. Life today is worth living. I am so glad to be out of the darkness that I used to live in. What I want most is to be able to inspire people in this life and to let the world know there are better days ahead. My story is real. This is my true testimony. If this story helps to save and inspire one person, then this book is worth writing.

I still have challenges in my life. Today, the difference is that I handle them without the use of drugs. Even the challenges in my life today will pass. One thing I learned is that as long as I don't pick up, I won't get high. That is something I take with me daily.

Today, I chose to stay drug-free. I will spend the rest of this life thanking God and showing my appreciation. Today, I thank the judge whom God used to enhance my life so that I could live a life of increase and further improve my quality of life. Today, I realize that action speaks louder than words, so I am choosing to reach out and help some-one in need.

My hope is for God to put me around a circle of friends and family whom I can be helpful. Today, I choose to stand up straight and treat myself like someone I am responsible for helping. I want to make friends with people who want the best for me. I compare myself to who I was yesterday, not to who someone is today, because everyone is different.

I will remain grateful and always give my testimony in the hope that it gives hope. Help is for those who want it, not need it. A part of my journey has been volunteering my time helping the homeless, donating clothes. This is a reminder of me.

I remember my dark days, and I often think about myself when I see the homeless. My heart tells me to do whatever I can. I look forward to doing it because it is my responsibility. People who find themselves in a dark place are still human beings. Kindness is what I needed in my dark days, and that is what I will also be—kind. I am not rich, but there are still ways I can help.

When I was out helping others, I would be a patient listener and share my knowledge of what worked for me. I would make sure not to pass judgment. I'd find myself talking to people nobody bothers to talk to, and I enjoy doing it.

As days pass, I realize there are so much more things that I could do to be of service to people. I remember when I first left rehab, I gathered up clothes and shoes and returned them to the rehab because there were people there who did not have visitors or family. I would always put myself in their shoes.

Today, I teach my kids and grandkids the importance of giving back. I teach them to never make fun of someone else's misfortune. Today, I practice compassion. I needed it in my time of pain and darkness, so I truly understand how important it is. I encourage my kids to do small acts of kindness toward other people. Today, I give out care packages to people I see on the street. God doesn't make mistakes. My journey that I have travelled was for me to become the kind of person who would give of herself. I didn't experience the things I went through that went unnoticed. It was simply so I could be the person whom God intends for me to be in this life.

Today, I find myself forgiving people who wronged me. I have been continuing to work on myself daily. It keeps me in a great space. I learned how to be open-minded, honest, and talk about things that I spent years of my life holding in. It helps me feel happier on the inside. I vent on a daily basis. I have had the chance to know what it feels like for someone to love you, regardless of the situation.

I feel that I have been trained to be able to give of myself. I do not regret my past as I look back. It had a meaning that I now understand. I remember at the beginning of my recovery when I would go to meetings. As I would hear people share their stories, I realized that we were family and we all had different stories, but the feelings were the same. That was when I knew I was in the right place. Family doesn't understand you like a person who has experienced certain traumas from drug addiction.

I felt right at home when I was at the meetings. It was also helpful for my kids when they would also go to the meetings with me. They also begin to see and learn about addiction. I have been able to make them proud of me, and that means the world to me.

I no longer live a life of being selfish and only thinking about myself. I am happy, and so are my kids. I am very grateful my grandkids are able to reap the benefits of my past. Everything I have learned and the knowledge I have. I share it with them.

Today, I take it easy as much as possible. I am good to myself. I love myself today. My hope is to wake up clean and free of drugs every day for the rest of my days. Me and my husband are happy in our marriage. We can finally sit back and enjoy our new home that God has allowed us to borrow. It really feels good to be in a new home after being addicted and homeless.

I will always remain teachable and never forget where I came from. I want God to put me in a position to do whatever it is that will be beneficial to someone else, so that people will remember me for the good I have done.

I believe that I will finally be walking in my passion. God always made a way for me because he knew this day would come. My prayer is for God to always keep me the way I am and keep me humble throughout my life ahead. I want to be great for someone who needs me on purpose because I feel like it is my job.

My prayer and belief are that God got me through this; there is nothing that God can't do. I will live with that and go do his work, as he would instruct my health, heart, and path. There is a purpose for every purpose.

Lord, I believe you intimately know the desires of my heart. Everything that I hope to achieve and become is known to you. Please guide me toward wise decisions and help me recognize when my paths are foolish.

Reveal to me when I need to realign my plans so that I may walk in step with your divine will and purpose for my life. In the name of Jesus, I pray. Amen.

About the Author

Danita Beckworth's purpose for writing this book is to let people in this world know that life can change regardless of what dark clouds come your way.